MW01675274

Chantil Thomas

SELAH

(Encounters)

AUSTIN MACAULEY PUBLISHERS™
LONDON • CAMBRIDGE • NEW YORK • SHARJAH

A CIP catalogue record for this title is available from the British Library.

ISBN 9781398422735 (Paperback)
ISBN 9781398422742 (ePub e-book)

www.austinmacauley.com

First Published 2022
Austin Macauley Publishers Ltd
1 Canada Square
Canary Wharf
London
E14 5AA

This book has been written to touch lives and impact individuals. For those who need hope and courage and stillness in a seeming chaotic and confusing time. To those who are struggling during tough times and for those who need encouragement to keep pushing through tough circumstances.

A dedication to my dad (1928–2021)

ACKNOWLEDGEMENTS

I would like to thank...

My mom and dad for inspiring me as parents to be a creative person. Without them I would not be the person that I am today.

My son Karl for his unconditional love towards me and being my sound board.

Karolina Kol for being available, even as a friend, to give input.

In memory of Leszek Czyżewski, our paths connecting at a time when I was writing this book.

Unathi Mbele, a young lady with tremendous creative potential, who helped me with illustrations.

I am thankful for every gift within every moment this life presents.

it's in the stillness that we HEAR
in the quiet place we are equipped

in the stillness that we SEE
in the quiet place it is revealed

in the stillness that we SENSE
in the quiet place we encounter

in the stillness we KNOW
in the quiet place we are known

in the stillness we TRUST
in the quiet place we are made whole

in the stillness we BECOME
in the quiet place we are released

so wait, in the stillness
trust in the quiet place

Steady my heart

Strength my heart

Listen to the sound of Heaven

Listen to the melody of LOVE

Hear my heart the beating in the stillness

The rhythm of this moment

This moment, this time, my heart be encouraged

Hear the echoes of joy and be glad

This bubbling let it find expression

And be the release

Courage, courage, Courage
I hear the Spirit sing, "Courage"
With songs that ignite the heart
And refresh the soul
Courage

Bring me your fears
Give me your tears
Entrust to me your anxieties
Let your hope rest in me
Courage

Son, take heart and be strengthened
Daughter, rest and let
Me love you
Into wholeness, to fulfil
My plans
Courage

I hear the Spirit sing over you
Courage, be strong and courageous

From a place of sensing the encouragement of the Lord. In times when I would be feeling discouraged and not so brave. When I'm wrestling with thoughts of self doubt and fear. Those moments when it almost cripples me to remain silent. When I'm encouraged to speak up and let my voice be heard. I hope you find your voice too!

You are crowned with jewels

Precious stones not known by man

You are royal

You are a diadem in the hands of the Master

The Creator, the Author of life

You are precious

You are irreplaceable

You are woven together

You are not a wanderer

You have been ordained with purpose

You are led in LOVE

For the splendour of the King

You are perfectly created

With your gifts, your talents and your treasures

"Purify, Purify"

Who shall ascend into the hill of the Lord

With clean hands and pure hearts

"Purify, Purify"

Let My people go

And let them come and prostrate to Me

I, yes, I alone am the Lord

"Purify, Purify"

Let the Priests come

And submit to the Altar

Raise up the sound of wailing and cry to Me

I, yes, I alone shall hear

And heal the lands

The Earth cries out, Creation in eagerness

For the sound of Trumpets

The call out for the Remnant

To rise up and STAND

"Purify, Purify"

O, come o come

The Lord Your God beckons you

He will come upon a cloud of Righteousness

Draped in crimson linen

Eyes burning like fire

Fire consuming, incinerating

Clearing the way of the Lord

Engulfing, paving the way for the

Bride In Victory, Triumphant

Arise, Daughter of Zion

Arise Son

Your King will come!

I'm reminded of a time, a day actually

When I woke up, feeling such resistance

Feelings of doubt, anxiety and uncertainty

Difficulty breathing the natural

Scent of my Heavenly Father's goodness

To be honest I did not feel much love

I could not hear the still voice

I could not recall even the blessings

That I knew deep down Jesus had given me

I just felt a push against who I was

And who Christ is in me!

Thoughts seem to be in unrest

As the contention between Truth and Lies arose

And even in the midst of such

A comfort overwhelms and I'm reminded

I am loved, I am kept, I am not alone

God will always redeem, even in my worst

Shepherd of my heart
Come, I cry out to You
Uncertainty, doubt and feeling fearful
What will tomorrow bring
Setting my gaze on the One who sets tomorrow
The One who holds time in His hands
The One who said "Light Be"
And there was light and the Earth became
The Heavens shaped by His breath
And into my nostrils He gave life

Shepherd of my heart
Counsellor in times of trials
The Anchor when the storms rage
The "stillness" to the winds bellowing
The One who knows me
He sees every thought, every desire He holds
My Shepherd, even when I walk through valleys,
He will guide me to the mountain top!

(.....)

Leaning into the heart of the Father
The heart of the Shepherd
Jesus, the Son, where the heart
of the Shepherd beats
To be where the Shepherd's heart aches

Hearts lost, searching crying out to the Shepherd
Connection, contact, where hearts in need
Searching to be aligned, in sync
Breathing the same life, the same LOVE
Refreshed, pressing into this wave
Waves and waves of the Father's thoughts
Towards these hearts abounds in compassion

Over oceans and seas in time
Each heart longing, receiving the heart
The perfection of the Father's embrace
I now receive, I am now made whole, I am now revived
I am now raised to LIFE!

In the darkness, Light came and from that Light,
Life was born

NTOMBI

My heart sings, my soul longs

For Your goodness, a depth of Your mercy

In the night time I wait on You

For the break of day I cling to You

Where shall I go;

Who do I have beside You

In Heaven and on Earth

My trust is in You alone

My redeemer, my Saviour, my Love

My soul years for You

In green pastures, You lead me

Stillness and quiet my resting place

Wake me from sleep

Slumber overwhelmed my being

Take me to Your heights

Where my feet will tread on high places

It is You I pursue

As You draw me even closer

Trust Is an Adventure

Trust when I cannot see

Trust when I don't know

Trust even when the darkness closes in

I can trust that I am not alone

Even when the winds stir in rage against me

Still I will trust

Trust the hope that is at work in me

Still I will trust the light that flickers

In the distant horizon

I will trust the glimmer of HOPE

I will trust the inner still voice

Calling me into the deeper parts

Of the ocean of Trust

and stills the fears in me

Trusting when I cannot see

Trusting when I don't know

Being Led by Love

LOVE comes to find me

LOVE pursues me into the uncertainty

LOVE beckons me into the deep

Deep whispers unto deep

“Come” LOVE surrenders

LOVE gives ALL

So LOVED the world

That LOVE gave and asked for my ALL

With holding nothing LOVE

Made known to me even its treasures

Laid bare for anyone who would accept

The gift, the submission, the pursuit of LOVE

Unto the world

LOVE comes to find

LOVE comes to secure

LOVE makes orphans as “SONS”

The Desert

Arid and barren spaces

Lifeless, breathless, a place of nothing

Chasing that which brings even more void

Where hearts are lost and crying for connection

A connection that soothes the pain, the fears of life

In this space steps in HOPE

In this place comes the springs of waters

In this place where once arid comes a song

A melody so great and intense

Like a flood comes the refreshing

Like an avalanche comes the burst of LIFE

Like the latter rain bringing COMFORT

Comes the deep wells of waters

Life giving waters to hearts thirsting, gasping

For the springs of LIFE even in the Desert

LIFE comes forth

"Like the African Savannah, after the storm, a once dry arid place, it will flower and flourish and give life. The beauty will arise.

Graham(RIP)

LIFE

The Earth longs for its Creator

Cries echo across barren lands

Desolation and abandonment

Streams once dried up

Now will revive

Dry bones scattered in the valley

Recovered and restored to life again

Once was lost now am found

Once was blind but now there is light

11/11 Divine alignment

There is a way set before man
There is a course that seems right
But filled with strive and struggles
It leads ultimately to death
The slow unconscious fate of the soul
There is a plan of Redemption
The Divine steps in and rescues
Setting in motion the resurrection
From death to live
From darkness to light
Once blind now with sight
Once lost now restored
No longer enslaved
From an orphan now called a son
Love has found its way
Capturing the stray
And brings home sons and daughters

Wait

I wait I wait for You

my heart waits for You alone

Like the Bride awaits her Groom

at the ceremonial dance

You call my name

You speak into my heart

Like the waters stirred You release a sound

Like the still and quiet waters You sing to me

A song of triumph and victory

Have you laid on my heart

Singing melodies of freedom

Rhythms of jubilation and a celebrating

And as the melody burst through my being

I dance with You my Lord, my King

The One my heart longs for

I wait, I wait, for You alone

Here I am!

Be immersed

Come and rest here

Come and put down the weights and the burdens

Let strive and worry cease

Come and rest from the rush of life

Breathing in the quiet and peaceful air

Refreshing waters, soothe the soul calming tranquil gently comforting

Wiping away tears

Drying up pain and grieve

Come and lay here

Put down the worry and strive

Come and take your place here

For you, there is enough

For you have so much

To come and find rest

I don't know if like me you get to places in your life where you experience tiredness. A tiredness that is so deep and profound that it alters your perspective and threatens to completely disengage you. And slump you into a nothingness of just existing. And because we are created for God and by God to have relationship and to be alive in Him, He will call us out of those grips and into a rest. A deep rest.

Void \ Without

(dedicated to everyone who sleeps on the streets)

shadows brutally confront
And expose the rage within
The pain, cut so deep
Bloodstained dreams and secrets

Alone, scared, afraid I watch as the world moves by
Does anyone care does anyone listen
Only the empty, cold whispers of the past I hear
Why this? Why me? What now?

"A plate of food, a cuppa tea, if you've got space a biscuit."
Drugged, doses increased, slumping my body in numbness
I feel nothing, no tears even come to bring release
I only sense the shadows, the coldness of the past haunts

Loudest only the voices that condemn and judge my existence
Why am I here? Does anyone care?
Do you see me? Do you know I have dreams?
Can you tell I need love?
Do you even understand the fears?

When you leave I'll still be here
You'll go back to your family
Love will wait to greet you
Warm and secured you lay down to sleep
While here on cold hard ground I wrestle within

Do you hear me? Do you care? Can you see me? Are you even there?

True to Self

People will ultimately engage with what's inside their hearts

And we gravitate towards that inside the heart

The fruits of what we see in people come from the seeds of the heart

How we perceive people may sometimes come from self perception

Love will always seek to serve the other

Just like breath life has many rhythms

When we stop we can better hear in the silence

Fear of losing control is ultimately fear of discovering true self

Truth of self is only truly found

In the stripping of what self holds precious, valued

Awake, awake, the depth of my soul

Awaken the melody, the sound

Stir the songs of LOVE

The One whom my heart thirsts for

In a place dry and weary, sing within

Songs of Awakening, re-birthing

Yet again, rise to LIFE

My soul burst out with shouts of JOY

Bubbling from inside, a great river

An endless stream of LIFE

In memory of Leszek Czyżewski

Even for a time people enter our lives
The time they stay and touch our hearts
Even for the time they get to impact us
The time they teach us to grow
Encourage us to step into unknown terrain
The moments we can cherish
The moments spent sharing
Whatever this gift be packaged as
However it may appear
These are the times in life we truly see people
We get to experience the unique melody of the heart
We get to acknowledge LIFE presented
We get to savour the gift granted
We get to appreciate the time spent
However that may be
Even for a time
Even for a season
Even for a reason
We sing in gratitude
We joy in thankfulness
Even when the time is over in this life
And this gift, this life, leaves this plain
It shall not forever disappear
It stays, it grows, it becomes
The gift now unwrapped, in the hearts of so many more
It will forever be
A precious pebble on the shore!

ABOUT THE AUTHOR

Chantil Thomas was born in Alexandra township, in Johannesburg, South Africa. She always enjoyed words, speaking, and writing since she was young. Writing poetry and short stories to make sense of her world and a space wherein she could give expression to her experiences. She is passionate about encouraging people and seeing people connect with their God-given identity and purpose and thereby journey life fully in all its expressions.

She is a mother of an amazing young man who constantly reminds her that life is an adventure. She is passionate about people, and seeing people live fully in who they have been created to be. In her own words, "the greatest gift you can give to the world is your true self." She hopes when people read her work, they will be inspired and find courage.

CPSIA information can be obtained
at www.ICGtesting.com
Printed in the USA
LVHW070925110222
710862LV00012B/384

9 781398 422735